RESCUING THE MILLENNIALS

Angeline,
To God Be the
Glory. Be Blessed!
Love You...

RESCUING THE MILLENNIALS

Essential Lessons Learned and Key Principles
to Reclaiming this Generation

Dr. Alethia J. Simmons

DR. ALETHIA J. SIMMONS

Xulon Press

Xulon Press
2301 Lucien Way #415
Maitland, FL 32751
407.339.4217
www.xulonpress.com

Scripture quotations taken from the King James Version (KJV) – *public domain.*

Scripture quotations taken from the Holy Bible, New International Version (NIV). Copyright © 1973, 1978, 1984, 2011 by Biblica, Inc.™. Used by permission. All rights reserved.

Printed in the United States of America.

ISBN-13: 9781545622704

TABLE OF CONTENTS

Dedication

"Honor your father and mother, so that you may live long in
the land the Lord your God is giving you."
Exodus 20:12(NIV)

This book is dedicated to the memory of my parents James and Sylvia Hill who taught me the importance of family love, support and relationships; the values and ethics of human worth for self and towards others; the significance of developing positive life-long community connections; the essence of academic excellence for wisdom and knowledge, and the Biblical principles for walking a Godly life. The lessons my parents taught were not only talked, but also demonstrated in their daily walk. They were both amazing human beings and their influence over my life has molded me to be the woman I am today. For this, I am eternally grateful. Thanks again Mom and Dad, the love in my heart for you will burn forever.

Acknowledgements

*"In everything give thanks; for this is
the will of God in Christ Jesus."
1 Thessalonians 5:18 (NKJV)*

Thank you Dr. Charlie Davidson and Dr. David Hirschman for sharing your expertise and leadership during my dissertation project. It was the thesis research that provided the foundation for this writing experience. I would like to thank my brothers Gary and Anthony for your unending love and support. I cherish the memory of two other siblings Michael and Judy who have already taken their flight to be with the Lord. Thank you to extended family members, friends, Rev. Patrick J. Walker and The New Macedonia Baptist Church members for your inspiration, prayers and sharing my happiness. A million thanks to Judy Lyons for rendering your proofreading expertise. I owe my greatest gratitude to my husband Joseph, son Aaron and grandson Isaiah for their faithful support, encouragement and love during this spiritual journey. I would have given up on this dream had they not had an influential impact on my life. Truly and foremost I am thankful to Jesus Christ for His vision, guidance, and loving kindness. Certainly without the Lord, none of this would have been possible. To God be the glory!

Prefaces

"If my people who are called by my name, will humble them-
selves, and pray and seek my face, and turn from their wicked
ways, then I will hear from heaven, and will forgive their sin
and heal their land." 2 Chronicles 7:14

What in the world is going on? Some people say that the church community is losing its affection, love, and wholesomeness. Others characterize the church as being dysfunctional and unhealthy. Many question the decline of membership and absence of millennials in the church. In 2016, I had the opportunity to visit nearly one hundred churches throughout the Washington, DC metropolitan area. In my travels, I noticed some churches flourishing, but many others had empty pews and dwindling congregations. I also observed that the population of baby boomers and elder congregants was increasing, while the number of millennials was decreasing. During this time, I had the opportunity to speak with many active churchgoers as well as others who had left the church. Most of those who had left the church indicated that the church no longer met their needs. While others seemed to be baffled and had no concrete answer or reason as to what has paralyzed the attendance and growth of the church. Hence, one common observation noted was…church is not the same, and many Christians are looking for a solution to get folks back into the church. Therefore, despite popular belief, the church as we know it today is in trouble. With all that is being said, it is apparent that a progressive intervention is necessary to curtail the dilemma that is presently upon the church.

I pose one question. What will cure this issue facing the church? Are you ready for the answer? The answer is quite simple. It is time for the church to wake up, go back to Christian principles, and fight the spiritual battle of destruction. The Apostle Paul beckons the body of Christ in Romans 13:11-14 (NIV):

> *And do this, knowing the time, that now it is high time to awake out of sleep; for now our salvation is nearer than when we first believed. The night is far spent, the day is at hand. Therefore, let us cast off the works of darkness, and let us put on the armor of light. Let us walk properly, as in the day, not in revelry and drunkenness, not in lewdness and lust, not in strife and envy. But, put on the Lord Jesus Christ, and make no provision for the flesh, to fulfill its lusts.*

When the church gets up and allows God to heal us from the inside out, we will be able and equipped to effectively minister to this lost and dying world. It is with humility that this book, **Rescuing the Millennials** is written to address the very critical topic that is facing the Christian church in America. This book will provide a training model to equip church leaders and anyone else interested in reaching the millennial generation with practical principles for reclaiming them. Therefore, without hesitation, it is urgent that the church step up as Apostle Paul admonishes us in Revelation 2:7, "He who has an ear, let them hear what the Spirit says to the churches."

Chapter One

Step One - Introduction

"I was glad when you said unto me;
Let us go into the house of the Lord."
Psalms 122:1

There was a time when folks were excited and glad to go to church. However, when you look at the state of the 21st century church, the future is not bright because of tremendous changes that have occurred over recent years. There has been much conversation about Americans and their lack of participation in the formalized church. Throughout this country, church attendance has become unpopular and membership has declined drastically. Over the past decades, decreasing attendance has been a common occurrence for many prominent churches regardless of denomination, theology, or worship style. Based on recent research, 65 percent of church membership is declining or plateauing. People in the American society have always attended church and been familiar with Biblical principles. However, as you look around today this is no longer the norm. In fact, there is a great change in the moral, social and spiritual lives of Americans. Consequently, many church doors have closed and pastors have resigned. Some popular mega-churches have lost their popularity because of high maintenance expenses for property and personnel. Due to social

1

changes, people are beginning to challenge the essence of God and the purpose for the church. Certainly, the American church and the future of Christianity are in a crisis. Therefore, it is important that a course of action be taken to ensure the survival of the church.

What Is Happening to the Church?

"You are severed from Christ, you who would be justified by the law; you have fallen away from grace."
Galatians 5:4(ESV)

Today, taking a closer look at this crisis, you find that the greatest decline of church membership and attendance worldwide is among young adults called millennials. This group of young adults born between the years 1981 and 2000 is embraced by a culture that has changed radically over the past decade. In years past, young adults would eventually reconnect with the church around the time they married and had children. However, today this is not the case. They are postponing marriage and child bearing until much later on in life. While returning back to church is not even part of their discussion. Certainly, this reflects a shift in the times. I am afraid that if issues are not addressed, the rate of churchlessness will continue to grow in America. Therefore, church leaders must get active in their efforts to address the current state of ministry. You need to come together, embrace a new way of "being the church," and move forward to bridge the gap of generational disengagement.

How do you bridge the gap?

"Be diligent to present yourself approved to God, a worker who does need to be ashamed, rightly dividing the word of truth." 2 Timothy 2:15 (NKJV)

The question is asked, "How do you bridge the gap of generational disengagement?" I'm glad that you asked. The answer is found within this Training Model which has been designed to prepare the church with practical principles to rescue the millennial generation. This training will address issues and trends that are relevant to churchlessness and the millennial generation. The model will prepare church leaders for change with commitment, confidence, self-assurance, and love. Change is Biblical, but unfortunately many churches struggle today in many ways because they refuse to alter their practices. Church leaders must serve as change agents. Jesus called for an inner change of the heart, which will produce a change in lifestyle (Luke 19:1-10). As the millennial generation changes, so must the church be prepared to meet the challenges of today's society.

The first section of this training will address and educate you on recent information regarding churchlessness as well as beliefs, practices, and directions for the millennial generation. A culmination of this information will summarize the lessons learned from research, surveys, and other pertinent literature. The second section will present a review of basic biblical principles that will provide an opportunity for leaders to receive a spiritual transformation. After the completion of this model, church leaders will be able to think more globally and discuss strategies for addressing some of the challenges. You will be able to formulate ways to bridge the gap for relationship development between the church and millennials. More importantly, you will be motivated with the tools that are necessary to design a plan of action for future implementation within your church.

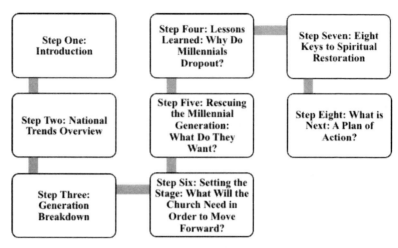

8 Steps - Training Model

Chapter Two

Step Two - National Trends

---

*"Take a census of all the congregation of the children of
Israel, their families, by their fathers' houses, according to
the number of names, every male individually."*
Numbers 1:2 (NKJV)

The Research Process

"My people are destroyed for lack of knowledge." Hose 4:6

*T*he purpose of this step is to present you with results
from a survey that I conducted as well as other highly
recognized research organizations regarding the millennial
generation. There is a great need to embrace research. You find
that social research is very necessary so that people are able to
receive a glimpse of trends, beliefs, practices and what is going
on around the country as it relates to certain issues. This information can be used to help you make wise decisions for future
endeavors. Also, throughout history, surveys are nothing new,
and they were taken during biblical times. The church can prepare for the return of the millennials by examining their concerns and desires for ministry as reported in data.

The research that I conducted ascertained information regarding the membership, participation, and program recommendations for millennials in the church. This survey solicited responses from pastors, youth/young adult leaders and churched/unchurched young adults who were born between the years 1981 and 2000. In summary, my research revealed that millennials are a generation without many inhibitions or fears; therefore, they will be unstoppable in the Kingdom of God. They are the church of the future. They will shape the church in powerful ways. More specifically, millennials state that they need the church to trust the God that is within them. They think that the church needs to listen, receive and help them carry out the dreams and visions that God has given them. Some feel that in order for them to move forward effectively, they will need to be equipped with the tools to do what God is calling them to do. Overall, the church needs to wake up, go forth and obtain practical approaches from lessons learned in order to develop effective principles to reclaim the millennial generation.

The Absence of Churches--the Failure to Attend

"Not forsaking the assembling of ourselves together, as is the manner of some, but exhorting one another, and so much the more as you see the day approaching." Hebrews 10:25

Churchlessness

Further research identified that the absence of churches or the failure to attend was categorized as churchlessness. Churchlessness is on the rise throughout the United States based on a recent study by the Barna Group. As the world evolves, it becomes less popular to attend church as it once was in previous years. One would ask, "What is churchlessness?" Wiktionary defines churchlessness as, "the absence of churches and the failure to attend a church."[1] Barna defines churchlessness as, "someone who has not attended a Christian church service, other than a special event such as a wedding or funeral, at any time during the past six months."[2] Church leaders cannot sit dormant and assume that the unchurched will eventually come back to worship. You must be proactive in your efforts to become more effective on how to unite and maintain connections with them.[3] It is an obligation of church leaders to understand the unchurched as well as fulfill the mandates established in Mathews 28:19 (NIV), "Therefore go and make disciples of all nations, baptizing them in the name of the Father and of the Son and of the Holy Spirit." If church leaders endeavor to bridge the gap that is prevalent between the churched and unchurched, they must make a concerted effort to understand their culture and learn to communicate with them.[4] As important, is the necessity to understand their pains, concerns, and desires? You need these components in order to develop worthwhile relationships. Research reveals:

> The Barna study divided the American group into four categories. The first group is identified as the *actively churched* who attend church at least once a month. They consist of 49 percent of the adult population. The second group that represents 8 percent of this population is called the *minimally churched*. They are unstable, but attend several times a year, showing up for special occasions and holidays such as Christmas, Easter, and Mother's Day. The third group represents 33 percent of this population and is called the *de-churched*. This group was once active in church, but now no longer attends. They appear to be the fastest growing group. The fourth group is called the *purely unchurched* who could possibly show a great increase in the future. They represent 10 percent

of the total population. The Barna study also revealed other interesting facts. There are more churchless men, but the percent for women is increasing. Most churchless people are single, white, and claim to be Christians.[5]

"On the other hand, the Pew Research Group identified that 20 percent of Americans have no religious connection. Within that group 33 percent of them are millennials. This finding totals approximately 33 million Americans who are unchurched." The Pew Research Center's Forum on Religion and Public Life conducted a study with the PBS television program, Religion & Ethics News Weekly. They found that even though this group is unchurched, they remained religious. Specifically, 68 percent of them believe in God, 58 percent are connected to nature and the Earth, 37 percent are spiritual, and 21 percent of them pray every day. Those who are spiritual believe in connecting with the dead, psychics, physical objects, yoga, and New Age practices. Their interest focuses on developing community relationships and helping the poor. They fault church leaders for being overly involved in money, politics, and power. Many of these groups are not interested in finding or connecting with a church.[6]

The Barna study showed another group called the *nones*. *Nones* claim no religious affiliations. This group identified that 56 percent of the *nones* are young males, 71 percent white, and 68 percent believe in God. They are strong Democrats, liberals, moderates, and Westerners.

Nones are supporters of the legalization of abortion and same-gender marriage.[7]

It is Time for the Church to Wake Up--

"Wake up, and strengthen what remains and is about to die, for I have not found your works complete in the sight of my God." Revelation 3:2 (ESV)

A Closer Look at the Millennial Generation

Research by the Pew Research Center also revealed that millions of millennials in America have left the church, but not their faith. The following demographic information on millennials was reported in an Executive Summary dated February 24, 2010.

> Generations, like people, have personalities, and millennials-the American teens and twenty-something's who are making the passage into adulthood at the start of a new millennium-have begun to forge theirs: confident, self-expressive, liberal, upbeat and open to change. They are more ethnically and racially diverse than older adults. They are less religious, less likely to have served in the military, and are on track to become the most educated in the history of America. Their entry into careers and first jobs has been set back by the Great Recession, but they are more upbeat than their elders about their own economic futures as well about the overall state of the nation.[8]

The Barna group conducted a national survey with millennials. Their responses were:

Two in five say church is not important because they can find God elsewhere (39 percent), and one-third say it's because church is not personally relevant to them (35 percent). One in three simply said church is boring (31 percent) and one in five say it feels like God is missing from church (20 percent). Only 8 percent say they don't attend because church is "out of date," undercutting the notion that all churches need to do for millennials is to make worship "cooler." A significant *number* of young adults have deeper complaints about church. More than one-third says their negative perceptions are a result of moral failures in church leadership (35 percent). Substantial majorities of millennials who don't go to church say they see Christians as judgmental (87 percent), hypocritical (85 percent), anti-homosexual (91 percent) and insensitive to others (70 percent).[9]

I found another nationally recognized group called The Life Way Research Team who had also conducted a study of 1,200 millennials in the United States. Their findings serve as the foundation for a book titled, *The Millennials: Connecting to America's Largest Generation*, written by Dr. Rainer and his son, Jess Rainer. The study found that,

Sixty-five percent of millennials identify themselves as Christian, while 14 percent say they are atheist or agnostic, 14 percent list no religious preference, and 8 percent claim other religions. Thirty-one percent of millennials pray by themselves at least once a day, while 20 percent never pray. Only 8 percent pray with others on a daily basis, compared with 65 percent that rarely or never pray with other people. Sixty-seven percent of millennials say they rarely or never read the Bible or other sacred writings. Only 8 percent read the Bible on a daily basis, although, in total, 21 percent do so at least once a week, and 34 percent do so at least once a month. One in four millennials attends religious worship services once a week or more, but two out of three rarely or never visit a church, synagogue, mosque, or temple. Twenty percent meet with others at least monthly in a small group to study the Bible, but 80 percent rarely or never do so. A slight majority (53 percent) disagree (strongly or somewhat) that the Bible is the written Word of God and is totally accurate in all it teaches.[10]

Praise God, despite what we hear, there are some millennials who still have a great love for Jesus Christ and their views on the church are positive. Their responses included:

Many say they attend church to be closer to God (44 percent) and more than one-third say they to learn more about God (37 percent). Some attend to get away from the stressfulness of daily life and to get the peace that is experienced in worship, prayer and teaching. Two-thirds of survey participants say that church is "a place to find answers to live a meaningful life." Over half say "church is relevant for my life" (54 percent), and about half "feel I can 'be myself' at church" (49 percent).[11]

Aren't you glad that all hope is not gone? Thank God King Solomon provides encouragement when he said, "Train up a child in the way he should go: and when he is old, he will not depart from it" (Proverbs 22:6). Therefore, no matter what the situation, or what statistical data reflects, you do not lose sight of the promises made by God. There is hope in Apostle Paul's message to the Corinthians as he noted,

> *So we do not lose heart. Though our outer self is wasting away, our inner self is being renewed day by day. For this light momentary affliction is preparing for us an eternal weight of glory beyond all comparison, as we look not to the things that are seen but to the things that are unseen. For the things that are seen are transient, but the things that are unseen are eternal. (2 Corinthians 4:16-18 ESV)*

In summary, as a result of all the research that I have studied, the most effective tool to reach the unchurched will be through love and kindness as cited in the book of Jeremiah, "With loving kindness have I drawn thee" (Jeremiah 31). Therefore, the church needs to understand the times, do not lose hope, and reach out to the churchless with love.

There is hope, let's get started—

"The Lord is all I have, and so in him I put my hope"
Lamentations 3:24(NIV).

With this said, certainly church leaders need to proceed in faith and be prepared to disciple the millennials, re-connect them with Christ, and then release them to their destiny in God. Hence, you must be flexible and adapt to the times that are prevalent in the world. In the meantime, as the world evolves, it is important that you remain consistent and grounded in basic Biblical principles.

For the most part, church leaders will have to find new ways to reach people wherever they are. ***"Methods are many,*** *principles are few, methods may change, but principles never do."*[12] Scripture declares, "Jesus is the same yesterday, today, and forever" (Hebrew 13:8). More importantly, it is necessary that you connect with God, so that His plan can be revealed. Therefore, if the church is to survive, you must take an immediate step to address this problem. In other words, it is time to recognize the times and begin to meet their needs. Jesus gives us a charge in Romans 13:11-14 (NKJV),

> *And do this, knowing the time, that now it is high time to awake out of sleep; for now our salvation is nearer than when we first believed. The night is far spent, the day is at hand. Therefore, let us cast off the works of darkness, and let us put on the armor of light. Let us walk properly, as in the day, not in revelry and drunkenness, not in lewdness and lust, not in strife and envy. But put on the Lord Jesus Christ, and make no provision for the flesh, to fulfill its lusts.*

Chapter Three

Step Three - Generation Breakdown

"The counsel of the Lord stands forever, the plans of His heart to all generations." Psalm 33:11 (ESV)

*T*he third step will present the generational characteristics of the Millennials, Baby Boomers, Generation
Xers, and the Elders. In order to bridge the gap between the
generations, you must be able to recognize and respect their
differences.

The Generations

The term *generation* is defined as "a group of people
defined by age boundaries—those who were born during a certain era. They share similar experiences growing up and their
values and attitudes, particularly about work-related topics,
tend to be similar, based on their shared experiences during
their formative years."[13]

All generations have different qualities and person-
ality traits. These traits are impacted by economic changes,
technology, and trends that influence generational changes
throughout American society. Generational differences can
affect how people relate and communicate with one another.
Therefore, it is important to understand and respect generational

characteristics in order to bridge the gap and develop positive relationships.

The four generational groups that I will discuss in this chapter are the Millennials, Generation Xers, Baby Boomers, and the Elders. The following diagram illustrates the name of each group, along with their birth dates.

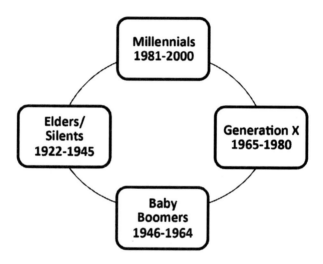

Four Generational Groups[14]

The characteristics of the Elder or the Silent Generation are:

- Born between 1922 and 1945
- Conformist, civic minded, and part of the great depression, World War II, and the Korean War
- Patriotic, 24 percent are veterans
- More than 24 percent attended college
- Men worked and the women stayed home to raise their families
- Some moved their families from farms and cities to the suburbs

- Very detailed and disciplined individuals
- Show ultimate respect for authority, conformity, and rules
- Focused on careers instead of activism
- Established many wealthy companies and developed space programs
- Hit by different illnesses such as dementia, Alzheimer, smoking, and alcoholism
- Created vaccines for polio, tuberculosis, etc.
- Began using estate planning, wills, and trust funds to establish long term security for their families.[15]

The characteristics of the Baby Boomer Generation are:

- Seventy-six million baby boomers were born between 1946 and 1964
- Emerged after World War II and ended around the time the birth control pill became available
- Goal-oriented and team builders
- Less traditional, but more tuned into social justices such as the right of abortion and homosexuality
- Advocates for equality and civil rights movement
- 44 percent of them have gay friends and family members
- More than 36 percent of them attended college and 54 percent work full time
- Around 13 percent of them are veterans and have even organized against the Vietnam War
- First to grow up with television and watched such programs as the Ed Sullivan Show, Happy Days, and American Bandstand
- Lived during era of rock and roll, transistor radios, Beatles, and the soul sounds of Motown
- Experienced life-changing events such as the gasoline shortage and the assassinations of President John Kennedy and Martin Luther King, Jr.

- A number of them control over 80 percent of personal financial assets, but 60 percent of them lost investments during the economic crisis
- Slower to make plans for retirement and establish long-term security plans for their families.[16]

The characteristics of Generation Xers are:

- 82.1 million Generation Xers were born between 1965 and 1980
- Known to be shrewd, yet well informed, highly educated, active, balanced, happy, and family oriented individuals
- Experienced school violence, bullying, peer pressure, and broken families
- Treated their parents as older friends and were pushed into adulthood early
- 6 percent of them are veterans, 49 percent of them attended college, 65 percent of them are employed full time, and others work as free agents
- Family incomes increased even though men made less and women worked more
- Based worldviews on social changes, abuse, and the outburst of HIV/Aids
- Have a passion for love, tolerance, and human rights for all
- Music videos and the sound of heavy metal emerged during this generation
- 46 percent of them have gay friends and family members
- The political arena during this era was incompetent, which resulted in the Watergate and Clinton-Lewinsky scandals
- Prefer to give their inheritance to charities rather than their children.[17]

The characteristics of the Millennial Generation are:

- 50 million millennials were born between 1981 and 2000
- Connected to one another more than any other generation because of electronics, technology, and gadgets
- Four out of ten of the millennials have one or more tattoos and one out of four has at least one body piercing
- Both parents raised six out of ten millennials
- The family is important to them and they have good relationships with their parents and their elders
- Tend to stay home longer
- Only one out of five of them are presently married
- Becoming the most educated generation in the history of America because of their accessibility to information
- Fifty-nine percent pursue post-secondary education
- Work ethics are not considered a priority; neither is fame nor fortune important
- Known to change jobs frequently
- 41 percent of them work full time due to the recession
- Team players and more radically diverse and tolerate of others
- Believe in helping the less fortunate and those in need
- Have homosexual or transgendered friends
- 60 percent of them favor same-sex marriage
- Greatly impacted by 9/11 and the Columbine High School shootings
- 2 percent of them are military veterans
- President Obama's greatest supporters.[18]

The president of The Barna Group, David Kinnaman divided the millennials into three groups: the *nomads, prodigals, and exiles*.[19] The first group called *nomads* represents four out of ten Christians who left and are no longer active in the church.[20] They declare a love for Jesus, but not for the church. The second group is called the *prodigals* and they represent one out of nine millennials who were raised as a Christian, but lost their faith.[21] They are determined to never return to church because many of them became disillusioned by church. They believe that Christianity no longer satisfies their desires. The third group, *exiles* include two out of ten millennials who feel stuck between the church and the world.[22] They want to be connected to society without giving up their faith.

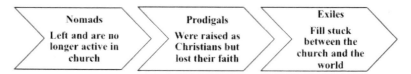

Nomads	Prodigals	Exiles
Left and are no longer active in church	Were raised as Christians but lost their faith	Fill stuck between the church and the world

Three groups of Millennials[23]

In summary, the following general characteristics can be considered for these groups when you compare their differences. The elder generation respects authority, while baby boomers are hopeful, Generation Xers are doubters, and the millennials are practical. The elders are traditional, baby boomers easily fall apart, Generation Xers are latchkey kids, and millennials believe in combined families. Educationally, the elders are dreamers, baby boomers believe in birthrights, Generation Xers seek ways to become more educated, and the millennials acquire incredible expenses. Over the past fifty years, society has gone from the rotary phone, to touch-tone phones, cell phones, and now the Internet, Skype, Twitter, Instagram, LinkedIn, and e-mails.[24] In summary, the attitudes of the generations have changed from working for everything to feeling entitled.

Consequently, technology has opened the door, which has allowed them to connect with new ways of learning and the world. Furthermore, millennials are more rebellious than former generations as opposed to being listeners and obedient to the laws of society. Previous generations received stronger corrective punishments whereas; today's action may come in the form of contemplation. Attention spans have decreased since the elder generation, whereas, constant reminders are needed to stay on task. Years past, marching was effective to protest unjust issues, but today Facebook is used to unify and advocate the same. Today, many handle confrontations with social media instead of using physical means. Today's challenge is to be flexible, while ascertaining, understanding and respecting generational differences, strengths, and weaknesses. The church is further charged to help the millennials identify their spiritual purposes. When this is achieved, subsequently church leaders can motivate them to step into place and pursue their destiny in God.

Conclusively, "Cultivating intergenerational relationships is one of the most important ways in which effective faith communities are developing a flourishing faith in both young and old. In many churches, this means changing the metaphor from simply passing the baton to the next generation to a more functional, Biblical picture of a body – that is, the entire community of faith, across the entire lifespan, working together to fulfill God's purposes."[25]

Chapter Four

Step Four - Lessons Learned: Why Do Millennials Drop Out?

"Let us hold fast the confession of our hope without wavering, for he who promised is faithful." Hebrews 10:23

The fourth step will present several reasons why millennials drop out of the church. Studies show that the decline in attendance reflects, "Younger members of society are being distracted because of their enormous work pressure and, with it, abundant choice for leisure, relaxation, and social activities."[26] Another possible reason for decreased church attendance by young adults is regarding their "postmodernist view, implying that they are more informed about products and services because of the greater accessibility of information."[27] Young adults are now in a position to decide whether or not they want to attend services, how often to do so, and even what type of church service they would prefer to attend.[28] Mark Taylor, a millennial expert who works with faculty to help them better connect with young people, suggests this movement is being driven by many college-age students who view organized religion as "strongly morally judgmental without accepting responsibility to accept truly 'religious' missions, like helping the poor and socially disenfranchised."[29]

Another reason why millennials indicate that they are leaving is because the church appears to be very controlling. Some feel that the church is evasive and does not deal with real life issues. A number of millennials feel that church is not connecting with them and their needs in today's society. Many millennials have not been able to find Jesus in the work of the church. Others disconnect because of the theoretical differences between Christianity and science. Some feel that the church should have progressive views on sexual matters. A few do not feel safe asking questions when they are in doubt about their Christian faith.

In principle, the unchurched person will not take the time to go to church. They would rather stay home, tune into their favorite station, and hear good worship music. Another major complaint they express for not attending church is that many of them believe Christians are hypocritical. They see people doing one thing in the church and living a complete opposite lifestyle outside the church. Consequently, when they do come to church, they are looking to see whether Christians are just going through the motions, or if they are truly sincere and real about their belief.

Leaders can prepare for the return of the millennials by examining the pitfalls of the church and concerns and desires that this generation has for ministry.

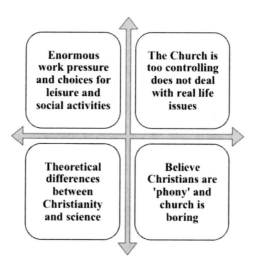

Lessons Learned: Why Do Millennials Drop Out of Church?[30]

24

Chapter Five

Step Five - Rescuing the Millennial Generation: What Do They Want?

"Delight yourself also in the Lord, and He shall give you the desires of your heart." Psalm 37:4

*S*tep five will cover what the millennials look for in a church. Research reveals that millennials want the church to be friendlier, so that they can experience an atmosphere of feeling welcomed and loved. They want the church to be real, honest, open, transparent, and accept the younger generation for who they are. Some want a church online. They want the church to become creative and incorporate technology into sermons and Bible sessions.

This generation wants the church to be Christ centered, where they are able to find and feel Jesus. They want to experience growth and develop deeper relationships with God and His people instead of participating in fancy programs. Others do not want to hear watered down sermons, but the simplistic Word of Jesus Christ. The millennials want a change in presentation style and not in substance. Some are not interested in entertainment and trimmings, but yearn to experience the presence of the glory of God. They wish to grow spiritually and challenged to live a Godly life, not just in sex, but honesty, caring for others, etc.

Millennials want a church that is committed to the family. They want to attend a church in their immediate neighborhood. This sense of community allows them to feel the closeness, warmth, and love that they experienced in their parent and grandparent's churches. They would like to know that their friends would be welcomed to attend church without fear of being ostracized or judged.

Millennials want a church that seeks to support outside causes through evangelistic efforts. They want to serve and volunteer where needed in their communities as well as globally. Millennials want to be able to participate and contribute in church activities. They want to be included in the decision making process of the church. This generation desires two-way lines of communication where they will be able to talk, listen, and feel free to ask questions. Most importantly, millennials want to glean wisdom from seasoned and senior saints.

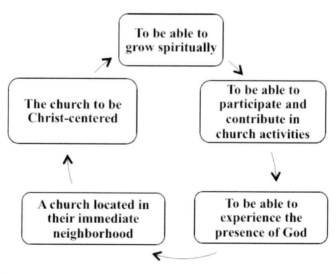

Rescuing the Millennial Generation:
What do they want from the church?

You will not be able to connect with millennials overnight. In fact, preparation is necessary. It will take a process of preparation, growth, and development over time. In addition, the different generations will need to develop relationships that depend on fellowship with Christ and how it influences other people with the power to bring about change.[31] "We learn from one another as together we learn from God."[32] It is my sincere prayer that all generations will join together, bridge the gap of separation and become better equipped, prepared, and divinely inspired with practical principles to reclaim the millennials.

Chapter Six

Step Six - Setting the Stage: How Does the Church Move Forward?

I will cry out to God Most High, to God who performs all things for me." Psalm 57:2

*S*tep Six will provide findings that I feel are necessary in order for the church to move forward. First, the church must be able to come together in corporate worship and cry out to God. David said, "The righteous cry out, and the Lord hears them; he delivers them from all their troubles" (Psalms 34:17). Throughout Scripture, God promises that he will hear a cry of distress, help, war, and a strong voice. Your cries will be heard when you are humbled, helpless, desperate, yielded, and sincere. God then answers these cries with healing, deliverance, victory, help, restoration, and revival.

After the church cries out corporately as well as individually, the Lord will renew your heart so that you can address the issues and concerns of the millennials. In order for this to happen the heart has to be prepared as David's was when he said, "Create in me a clean heart, O God, and renew a steadfast spirit within me" (Psalms 51:10). The heart is the seat of the mind, will, and emotions. Your heart must be ready to be able to glorify God, so that you can submit to God and His plans, and seek the Savior's honor. Solomon said, "The preparation of the heart belongs to man, but the answer of the tongue is from the Lord" (Proverbs 16:1). The Lord states in His Word that He will renew the heart and fill it with new desires, purposes, affections, and joy. Ezekiel wrote, "I will give you a new heart and put a new spirit in you; I will remove from you your heart of stone and give you a heart of flesh" (Ezekiel 36:26).

The Lord promised to heal His people if they followed His instructions as mentioned in 2 Chronicles 7:14. Many people in the church are suffering due to mental, physical and spiritual illnesses. They must get well in order to be effective witnesses to others. Therefore, this act of obedience will bring forth revival, restoration and a renewed spirit, which will be necessary in order to have an open mind to minister to the millennial generation.

What Will the Church Need in Order to Move Forward?

Another question asked, "What will the church need in order to move forward?" The church will need spiritual discipline to move forward. Spiritual discipline is an inner attitude of the heart that brings people into reality with their spiritual life.[33] Spiritual change occurs as God is allowed to transform you through the following sources: worship, prayer, meditation, fasting, repentance, Scripture, discipleship, fellowship and love. The closer people come to the heartbeat of God, the more you will see their needs and have a desire to be conformed like Christ.[34] The church should model the spiritual aspects of true Christianity. Actions speak louder than words; therefore Christians should be able to live, as Jesus would want you to do. James declares, "Do not merely listen to the word, and so deceive yourselves. Do what it says" (James 1:22).

The Prodigal Son

The parable of the Prodigal Son will serve as one of the foundational Scriptures for which the keys for church preparation will be based. The story of the Prodigal Son according to Luke 15:11-32, begins when he asks his father for an early inheritance. The father honored his son's wish, but his son soon lost it all with lavish living. Shortly thereafter, a famine hit the land and the son was forced to take a job working with swine. He became very hungry yet no one would give him anything to eat. At this point he realized how foolish he had been. Specifically, Scripture says that he came to his senses, "But when he came to himself" (Luke 15:17). He later decided to go back home, repent to his father, and volunteer to work as his servant. The father looked up, saw his son coming back home, ran out to meet him, and gave him a big kiss. Before the son could finish repenting, his father began to shower him with gifts and plan a big celebration. The son that had always been home became very angry about the celebration. At this point, it was not about the son that had stayed home, but the other son who had been lost and now found.

First, as the parable is reviewed, it was very disrespectful for the son to ask for his birthright prior to the death of his parents. Despite this custom, the father did not rebuke him, but gave the son his inheritance. Second, even after the son squandered his inheritance and returned home, his father never pressured him, but received him back with a forgiving heart, gifts, and a celebration feast. As you reflect on this parable, you will see that the Father is symbolic of God who is love, patience, and compassion. God is the perfect example for earthly fathers. On the other hand, bitterness kept the older son from forgiving his brother. In essence, the older son represented the self-righteous Pharisees who had forgotten to celebrate when the lost returns to God with a forgiving heart. The act of humility from the father and resentment from the younger son serves as a model for how to respond to those who repent and return to God. Therefore, the behavior of the older son shows what should not be displayed when the millennials return to God. Most importantly, the father models the love that should be shared with those who return home.

In summary, aren't you glad that the Lord continues to bestow grace with His mercy and never treats us the way we deserve to be treated? The story supports Scripture where it is stated that God will give those who left Him a heart to return back home. As recorded in Jeremiah 24:7, "I will give them a heart to know me, for I am the Lord; and their God, for they will return to me with their whole heart." In addition, the characteristics that were displayed by the father in this parable will serve as the keys that will prepare church leaders to connect with the millennials when they return to the church. What role will the church play in this effort? Will you take on the attitude of the oldest son who was angry and unforgiving? Certainly not, you will model the father who seeks to bring restoration to his son through love.

In essence, the church must be flexible so that they will be prepared to disciple the millennials back to Christ and ready to accept them where they are with joy and a loving heart.

Chapter Seven

Step Seven - Eight Keys to Spiritual Restoration

"Restore to me the joy of your salvation,
and uphold me with a willing spirit."
Psalm 51:12 (ESV)

*S*tep seven will cover the spiritual disciplines that I consider will transform God's people. These disciplines include: *worship, prayer, meditation, fasting, repentance, Scripture, discipleship, fellowship and love.* The closer people come to the heartbeat of God, the more they will see their needs and have a desire to be conformed like Christ.[35] You must search your heart to determine whether you have had a true experience with God. Others will see that God is real because they will see the power demonstrated. Without the evidence of God's genuineness, the church will be inefficient in their attempts to reach the world. Likewise, you must prepare for change, be intentional in developing relationships, and move to develop a plan of action that will incorporate the wisdom of the old and strength of the young.

This is not the first time that people left the church--

Ironically, history has a tendency to repeat itself. There were many periods throughout history when people became unchurched and left their faith. One such time was in America when they experienced a spiritual and economic decline after the American Revolution. Because of war, many church leaders were killed, homes and farms were destroyed, and church membership declined. People turned their faces away from God, deism spread throughout the land, and sin became prevalent. One church historian wrote, "It seemed as if Christianity were about to be ushered out of the affairs of men."[36] The author wrote, "What was the cure? How could any kind of spiritual antidote be applied to this dreadfully sinful disease?" According to Orr, the cure came through a "concert of prayer."[37] People began to fervently pray, and as a result, revival hit the land. Thousands of those who attended these revivals surrendered their lives to Christ, while others returned and renewed their faith. They continued to have corporate prayer and fasting meetings.

During this same period, camp meetings surfaced and thousands of people traveled from faraway places to gather in outdoor settings to hear the Gospel of Jesus preached by fiery preachers. The Holy Spirit moved in such a powerful way that church memberships within the Methodist and Baptist churches grew by the thousands, and hundreds of churches were formed. Not only did revival spread throughout America, but abroad as well. The Great Spiritual Awakening manifested a change. It also ignited the birth of several Bible societies, a missionary society, and Sunday school.[38] Great revivals, camp meetings, evangelistic campaigns, and movements continued throughout the years, and they were all manifested by the word of prayer. If God did it then, He can certainly do it now. The Scripture confirms, "Jesus is the same yesterday and today and forever" Hebrews 13:8 (KJV).

Hence, restoration of the church and its people will come through prayer. Another example of this promise of restoration is found in the book of 2 Chronicles. The story is recorded when the Lord gave King Solomon a warning after he built the temple. The Lord advised Solomon that His blessings were conditional, but gave him a promise in the following prayer, "If my people, which are called by my name, shall humble themselves, and pray, and seek my face, and turn from their wicked ways; then will I hear from heaven, and will forgive their sin, and will heal their land" (2 Chronicles 7:14). God called to His people and the church to do four things: *humble themselves, pray, seek His face, and turn from their wicked ways.* Then, God told Solomon that if the people were obedient and did these four things, He will hear from heaven, forgive their sin, and heal their land. This is the promise for today, having faith that God will bring healing, deliverance, and restoration to those who are lost.

You must remember, as mentioned in previous chapters, reputable groups and companies conducted numerous studies, which identified the millennials concerns, issues, and problems centered on the church and their involvement. Therefore, do not forget to study the results of research in order to know what specific issues you need to address. Of course, this cannot be executed effectively without going first to God. Once you have accomplished this step, you are ready to move forward to achieve spiritual restoration.

Eight Keys for Spiritual Restoration

The future of the 21st century church is dismal. Therefore you must take immediate action to address the critical decline in church membership and participation among the millennial generation. Many have suggested that the church needs to return to basic and simplistic principles. The keys that you must use to prepare the church will be Biblical principles. Spiritual principles are the truths that you need for living a Christian life. The Holy Spirit empowers these principles. Spiritual principles are found throughout Scripture and provide the ingredients that you need to grow and mature in a relationship with God. I identified spiritual principles in the parable of the Prodigal Son found in Luke 15 and the prayer spoken in 2 Chronicles 14. These principles include; *love, prayer, humility, seeking the Lord, worship, repentance, and the Word of God.* These principles will prepare the church to be restored, strengthened, and released to move forward to develop relationships and sensitivity towards the needs and concerns of the millennial generation. As the principles are studied and meditated on corporately and individually, leaders will be renewed into an oneness with God. This oneness will enable you to be obedient and follow His instructions. The process of spiritual renewal will not happen overnight, but change will occur through continual diligence and faith.

Keys for Spiritual Restoration

Key 1: Love

Love is the main component in this model to prepare the church for the return of the millennial generation. All other keys are centered on the foundation of love and will not be effective without the other. It is written in Ephesians 4:2-3, "With all humility and gentleness, with patience, bearing with one another in love, eager to maintain the unity of the Spirit in the bond of peace." Likewise, Apostle Paul wrote to the Corinthians and said, "And though I have the gift of prophecy, and understand all mysteries and all knowledge, and though I have all faith, so that I could remove mountains, but have not love, I am nothing" (1 Corinthians 13:2). Remember in the parable of the Prodigal Son, it was because of love from the father that he was able to receive his son back home with compassion, forgiveness, gifts, and a celebration. You as church leaders have to be ready and prepared to effectively minister to the millennial generation in love when they return. If you are not ready, the millennials will either go to another church or back out into the world. The Lord spoke to Jeremiah and said, "The Lord has appeared of old to me, saying, Yes, I have loved you with an everlasting love; therefore with loving kindness I have drawn you" (Jeremiah 31:3). Paul also wrote to the Corinthian church,

Love suffers long and is kind; love does not envy; love does not parade itself, is not puffed up; does not behave rudely, does not seek its own, is not provoked, thinks no evil; does not rejoice in iniquity, but rejoices in the truth; bears all things, believes all things, hopes all things, endures all things. Love never fails. However, whether there are prophecies, you will fail; whether there are tongues, you will cease; whether there is knowledge, it will vanish away. (1 Corinthians 13:4-8 NKJ)

God's love is made up of four attributes: *benevolence, grace, mercy, and persistence.*[39] The first attribute, *benevolence* is an unselfish concern and care for others to include friends, neighbors, and even enemies. The Lord demonstrated His greatest love towards mankind when he proclaimed, "For God so loved the world that He gave His only begotten Son, that whoever believes in Him should not perish but have everlasting life" (John 3:16). The second attribute is *grace* which God provides man with His goodness, not based on what he deserves, but because of their needs.[40] The third attribute is *mercy*, "God's mercy is His tenderhearted, loving compassion for His people. It is His tenderness of heart toward the needy."[41] Jesus traveled "teaching in their synagogues, preaching the good news of the kingdom and healing every disease and sickness" (Matthew 9:35-36). The last attribute is *persistence*, which includes long-suffering and patience.

Key 2: Humility

An important attitude mentioned in Scripture is *humility*. Humility is defined as being grounded in the character of God. First, God exalted Jesus and in turn He exalted man. According to the book of Philippians, "Wherefore God also hath exalted him, and given him a name which is above every name: that at the name of Jesus every knee should bow, of things in heaven, and things in earth, and things under the earth" (Philippians 2:9-10). Jesus placed a great emphasis on humility and taught lessons on it throughout the Bible. Humble people see themselves as being small before God and man. He owes his very existence to the grace of God. It is written in Philippians 2:5-8 (ESV),

> *Have this mind among yourselves, which is*
> *yours in Christ Jesus, who, though he was in*
> *the form of God, did not count equality with*
> *God a thing to be grasped, but emptied himself,*

by taking the form of a servant, being born in the likeness of men. In addition, being found in human form, he humbled himself by becoming obedient to the point of death, even death on a cross.

A humble man is also excited about the positive strengths and welfare of others. You are humble towards one another. Apostle Peter wrote in 1 Peter 5:5 (ESV), "Likewise, you who are younger, be subject to the elders. Clothe yourselves, all of you, with humility toward one another, for God opposes the proud but gives grace to the humble." The test of humility is when you are able to become humble before God as well as man. Paul writes to the Romans and says, "Be of the same mind toward one another. Do not set your mind on high things, but associate with the humble. Do not be wise in your own opinion" (Romans 12:16 NASB).

The steps of humility are:

Steps of Humility	Scripture Reference
Fear the Lord.	"By humility and the fear of the Lord are riches and honor and life" Proverbs 22:4).
Humble yourself in His presence.	"Humble yourselves in the sight of the Lord, and He will lift you up" (James 4:10).
Acknowledge your sins.	"For we all stumble in many things. If anyone does not stumble in word, he is a perfect man, able also to bridle the whole body" (James 3:2).

| Take wrong patiently. | "Finally, all of you be of one mind, having compassion for one another; love as brothers, be tenderhearted, be courteous; not returning evil for evil or reviling for reviling, but on the contrary blessing, knowing that you were called to this, that you may inherit a blessing" (1 Peter 3:8-10). |
| Submit to authority. | "Servants, be submissive to your masters with all fear, not only to the good and gentle, but also to the harsh" (1 Peter 2:18 NKJV). |

The results of Humility are:

Results of Humility	Scripture Reference
The Lord adorns the humble with salvation.	"For the Lord takes pleasure in His people; He will beautify the humble with salvation" (Psalm 149:4 NKJ).
The humble will receive wisdom.	"When pride comes, then comes shame; but with the humble is wisdom" (Proverbs 11:2 NKJ).
The Lord will exalt the humble.	"Humble yourselves in the presence of the Lord and He will exalt you" (James 4:10 NASB).
Others will acknowledge sins.	"You will gain wealth and honor, and the fear of the Lord bring wealth and honor and life" (Proverbs 22:4).

True humility exists when you die completely to yourself and depend solely on the power of the Holy Spirit. It is at the point of sincere lowliness that you become a vehicle to manifest the divine glory of God.

Key 3: Prayer

The next key is prayer. The Lord instructs us to pray, "Then He spoke a parable to them, that men always ought to pray and not lose heart" (Luke18: 1). Prayer is communicating with God in simple everyday language. It is written in Matthew 6:7, "And when you pray, do not use vain repetitions as the heathens do. For they think that they will be heard for their many words." Prayer allows you to talk to God, develop, and maintain a close relationship with Him. It gives you an understanding of His Word and enables you to reproduce after His character. According to Apostle Paul writing to Timothy, "I urge, then, first of all, that petitions, prayers, intercession and thanksgiving be made for all people, for kings and all those in authority, that we may live peaceful and quiet lives in all godliness and holiness. This is good, and pleases God our Savior, who wants all people to be saved and to come to a knowledge of the truth" (1 Timothy 2:1-4). "Prayer is intimacy with God that leads to the fulfillment of His purpose." The Holy Spirit will teach you how to pray, "Likewise the Spirit also helps in our weaknesses. For we do not know what we should pray for as we ought, but the Spirit Himself makes intercession for us with groaning which cannot be uttered" (Romans 8:26).

You can bring ordinary concerns directly to God when the prayer is simple and from the heart. When you meet the Father, you are able to fall into His arms and He in turn sings sweet love songs to you. He leads you to a deeper understanding and practices of prayer, which allows you to become closer to Him, to yourselves, and to your community.[42] Jean-Nicholas Grou says, "It is the heart that prays, it is to the voice of the heart that God listens and it is the heart that he answers."[43]

Jesus often shared and modeled the importance of prayer with His disciples. He was very passionate and consistent. The ministry of the disciples was birthed in prayer.[44] "Prayer is not a preface or an addendum to the work of ministry. It is the work of the ministry."[45] A powerful prayer to begin with is the Lord's Prayer. Jesus taught His disciples in this manner,

> *Our Father in heaven, Hallowed be your name. Your kingdom come. Your will be done on earth as it is in heaven. Give us this day our daily bread. And forgive us our debts, as we forgive our debtors. And do not lead us into temptation, but deliver us from the evil one. For yours is the kingdom and the power and the glory forever. Amen. (Matthews 6:9-13)*

The Lord's Prayer, often called the model prayer was written with great influence. It was designed so that you could go into the heart of God to recognize who He is and what He has done for us. As the Lord's Prayer is accepted, the church must first obey the instructions on how to approach God who is the Father.[46] Jesus has given the invitation to "come unto me" (Matthew 11:28). The "Father seeks such to worship him" (John 4:23). There is access to Christ as you approach His throne. "You have immediate access to him who is everywhere" (Psalm 139:8). There is an intimate and oneness with God when you make Him real in your heart. He is concerned about the needs of the church and demands that you obey and give Him reverence. When this is done, then the glory of God will be revealed in the midst of the local church, life trials, and tribulations.[47] In this, the attributes of God are recognized. He is found to be "merciful, gracious, long-suffering, abundant in goodness and truth, and forgiving of sin" (Exodus 34:6-7).

There are other types of prayers that you can use which depend on the issue or situation. Just a few include,

Type of Prayers	Scripture Reference
Faith and Mercy Prayers	"Let us then approach God's throne of grace with confidence, so that we may receive mercy and find grace to help us in our time of need" (Hebrews 4:16 NIV).
Receiving Prayers	"Therefore I tell you, whatever you ask for in prayer, believe that you have received it, and it will be yours" (Mark 11:24 NIV).
Trust and Reliability Prayers	"The Lord is near to all who call on him, to all who call on him in truth" (Psalm 145:18 NIV).
Understanding Prayers	"Call to me and I will answer you and tell you great and unsearchable things you do not know" (Jeremiah 33:3 NIV).⌡

Foremost, when prayer is released, the glory of God is effective. When prayer is passionate, transformation takes place personally and corporately. God wants you to praise and give Him glory. As mentioned previously, there have been great revivals because of prayer. These revivals released spiritual explosions worldwide. As a result, "thousands of people turned from sinful behavior to embrace righteousness and holy living. Broken lives were mended and crushed relationships were restored."[48]

Key 4: Seek the Lord

God invites His people to seek Him. "But seek first the kingdom of God and His righteousness, and all these things shall be added to you" (Matthew 6:33). When you actually see God and His awesomeness, all of the attention leaves away from self. There develops a longing to reverence Him, just because He is holy. Eventually, you get a connection of intimacy with God and attain an assurance of His love.

In addition, meditation is very important and should be a part of your prayer and worship. The purpose of meditation is to get still before the Lord so that you can hear and understand what He is speaking into your spirit. Once you receive your instructions from Him, then you are free to go forth and follow His commands. Therefore, because of your obedience, you will have good success in what you do. The Lord gave Joshua specific instructions for leadership after the death of Moses when he said, "This Book of the Law shall not depart from your mouth, but you shall meditate on it day and night that you may observe to do according to all that is written in it. For then you will make your way prosperous, and then you will have good success" (Joshua 1:8). At this point, when you have totally surrendered to God, there is peace and an assurance through faith that He will provide and handle your every need.

Key 5: Worship

Worship is described as "The loving ascription of praise to God for what He is both in Himself and His ways. It is the bowing of the innermost spirit in deep humility and reverence before Him."[49] The Lord seeks true worshipers. David proclaims in (John 4:23 NIV), "Yet a time is coming and has now come when the true worshipers will worship the Father in the Spirit and in truth, for you are the kind of worshipers the Father seeks." Biblical worship encompasses your heart and love of God to worship Him in spirit and in truth.[50]

Through the centuries, there have been periods of great encounters with God."[51] These experiences were called revivals or Great Awakenings. God used a host of people to usher in innovations that still impact the way you express corporate worship. Such men as Moody and Sankey contributed to "worship evangelism" by moving outside the walls of the church to reach the unsaved. During these periods of awakening, new methods, styles, processes, and techniques of worship emerged.[52] Sometimes God's people emerged from awakenings expressing their love for Him in completely new ways. When church members experienced such awakenings, their lives were always changed, communities were transformed, families were restored, and people turned from wickedness to righteousness.

The church has experienced many innovative ways to worship God. God is not just calling for better worship, but a personal relationship with him.[53] In the book of Philippians it states, "I want to know Christ—yes, to know the power of His resurrection and participation in His sufferings, becoming like Him in His death" (Philippians 3:10 NIV). True knowledge of Christ alters and changes man, their judgments, manners, and makes them brand new. "Being the crown of God's creation, worship was created deep inside the heart of man. God wanted a vibrant relationship with His best creation and desired to dwell with those He loved. He not only wants us to have a worship life, but God wants us to have Him" (Philippians 3:10 NIV). Worship is in the heart of men, women, and every movement of God. You will grow when your attitude and practice of worship becomes a daily lifestyle and reflects the character of God.

Key 6: Repentance

Repentance means to feel sorrow over sin and turn away in both the mind and heart from self to God. Ezekiel 18:30 states, "Therefore, O house of Israel, I will judge each one according to His way, declares the Sovereign Lord. Repent! Turn away from all your offenses; then sin will not be your downfall." It was a command from God that all people repent so that you would be able to see and enter into the Kingdom of God, Acts 17:30, "Truly, these times of ignorance God overlooked, but now commands all men everywhere to repent." Then Jesus said, "The time has come. "The kingdom of God is near. Repent and believe the good news" (Mark 1:15). A call to repentance is found in Hosea 6:1-3(ESV),

> *Come, and let us return to the LORD; For He has torn, but He will heal us; He has stricken, but He will bind us up. After two days He will revive us; on the third day He will raise us up, that we may live in His sight. Let us know; Let us pursue the knowledge of the LORD. His going forth is established as the morning; He will come to us like the rain, like the latter and former rain to the earth.*

Key 7: Fasting

Throughout the history of the Bible, fasting along with prayer has proven to be extremely beneficial and necessary for church development. It is a skill to learn, an art to acquire, and an ability that needs to be trained. The greatest reason to fast is to get to know God and to feed on the Bread of Life. When you fast, you begin to sample God by praying and listening to him. One of the primary purposes of fasting is to provide healing and rest for the body.[54] Because of fasting, the body is detoxified and rid of both physical and spiritual impurities.

Moreover, fasting will enable your faith and trust to grow in God. Your spiritual authority in the Holy Spirit will be increased. It will provide divine guidance, direction, and affirmation of ministry. Fasting will give spiritual insights during Bible study, enhance your desire to pray, and increase a personal sense of God's presence.[55] As important, with the increase of demonic activity throughout the world, you will witness an assurance of divine protection and have victory over satanic strongholds.[56] When time is spent with God in prayer, you will find that a new spiritual hunger replaces the old physical desire. As important, when the secret art of fasting is found in the heart of God, you will get the victory in Jesus and enjoy His peace.[57] Fasting takes on additional facets other than the absence of food. True fasting includes planning, preparation, and purposely seeking the Lord. The process of fasting includes:

Fasting Objectives	Scripture References
God's Intervention	"David pleaded with God for the child. He fasted and spent the nights lying in sackcloth on the ground" (2 Samuel 12:16 NIV).
Repentance	"When they had assembled at Mizpah, they drew water and poured it out before the LORD. On that day they fasted and there they confessed, We have sinned against the LORD" (1 Samuel 7:6).
Guidance	"Paul and Barnabas also appointed elders in every church. With prayer and fasting, they turned the elders over to the care of the Lord, in whom they had put their trust" (Acts 14:23 NLT).

Key 8: Study the Word of God

The job of church leaders is to spiritually challenge, instruct, and refresh the congregation through practical Bible teaching. The Word, who was God, has been around since creation. Apostle John noted, "In the beginning was the Word, and the Word was with God, and the Word was God" (John 1:1). God inspired Scripture that was given to man for wisdom, so that he would be complete and ready to do a good job for Him. Apostle Paul wrote, "And that from childhood you have known the Holy Scriptures, which are able to make you wise for salvation through faith which is in Christ Jesus. All Scripture is given by inspiration of God, and is profitable for doctrine, for reproof, for correction, for instruction in righteousness, that the man of God may be complete, thoroughly equipped for every good work" (2 Timothy 3:15-17).

The Word of God will judge the thoughts and attitudes of the heart. Paul states, "For the Word of God is alive and active. Sharper than any double-edged sword, it penetrates even to dividing soul and spirit, joints and marrow; it judges the thoughts and attitudes of the heart" (Hebrews 4:12 NIV). God speaks to His people through the Bible. Also, the Scriptures give us patience and comfort. "For whatever things were written before were written for our learning, that we through the patience and comfort of the Scriptures might have hope" (Romans 15:4 NKJV). The Bible provides spiritual food on the truths of faith.

When prayer is united with the Word of God, it generates boldness in our life. "After you prayed, the place where you were meeting was shaken. And you were all filled with the Holy Spirit and spoke the Word of God boldly." Whenever the evil one confronts you, the Word of God will make you strong. It is written in 1 John 2:14 (NIV), "I write to you, dear children, because you know the Father. I write to you, fathers, because you know Him who is from the beginning. I write to you, young men, because you are strong, and the Word of God lives in you, and you have overcome the evil one." For the most part, the Word of God is completely reliable, enlightening, and direct. It will guide you through darkness to all truths. David said, "Your Word is a lamp to my feet and a light to my path" (Psalms 119:105).

In summary, the good news is that the Lord can turn any situation around. No matter what people say or statistics reflect, there is nothing impossible with God. "For with God nothing will be impossible" (Luke 1:37). God is coming to repossess His church, but you have to be hungry for this to happen. Every good thing that the church does should flow from the presence of God. He wants you to dwell with Him in intimate communion, but the flesh must first die.[56] You can be so caught up in being "religious" that you never become spiritual. It is time for the church to experience the glory and presence of God. "The next wave of true revival will bring waves of unchurched people. When you hear that there is fresh bread in the house, you will run through the doors after smelling the fragrance of God."[57]

Chapter Eight

Step Eight - What is Next: A Plan of Action?

"Write the vision and make it plain on tablets, that he may run who reads it." Habakkuk 2:2

*W*hat is next? Step eight will guide church leaders to design a Plan of Action. This eight-step model will help you enhance organization management, set priorities and acquire the resources needed to achieve your goals.

8 Steps – Plan of Action	
Step 1	Humble yourself, seek the face of God – begin in prayer
Step 2	Identify a work team – continue in prayer
Step 3	Analyze data and research results – stay in prayer
Step 4	Write vision, goals and objectives – endure in prayer
Step 5	Establish strategies and procedures – carry on in prayer
Step 6	Determine a time frame and resources needed – sustain in prayer

Step 7	Launch the plan – proceed in prayer
Step 8	Assess and revise plan – remain in prayer

Humans are limited, but God is the final authority regarding all religious matter. God has established the principles, beliefs, and practices that Christians must follow. God's directives are found in the Bible, which is the vehicle by which He speaks. "The Biblical view is that God is guiding history to His goal and that we can have assurance that if we align ourselves with His purpose, we will be moving to an assured outcome of history."[58] It is written in Proverbs 19:21 that "Many are the plans in a man's heart, but it is the Lord's purpose that prevails."

The work of the Holy Spirit in a Christian's life is a continuous process. The Holy Spirit empowers a believer to do the work of the Lord. John 14:12 states, "Most assuredly, I say to you, he who believes in me, the works that I do he will do also; and greater works than these he will do, because I go to my Father." Whatever the instructions are that God has assigned, He has already given you the power to fulfill it.

Therefore, since the assignment is from God, He has the directions and strategic plan of action. To execute God's plan, it is necessary for you to walk in the Spirit. Hence, the Holy Spirit will guide you into all truths as written in John 16:13-14, "However, when He, the Spirit of truth, has come, He will guide you into all truth; for He will not speak on His own authority, but whatever He hears He will speak; and He will tell you things to come. He will glorify me, for He will take of what is mine and declare it to you." As you walk in the Spirit, God will produce the fruit of Spirit within you, "But the fruit of the Spirit is love, joy, peace, longsuffering, kindness, goodness, faithfulness, gentleness, and self-control" (Galatians 5:22-23). You will never be successful in fulfilling God's plan without the manifestation of the fruit of the Spirit. So, the fruit of the Spirit needs to be renewed so that God can reveal His plan for uniting and working with the next generation.

Small Group Discussion Sessions

As a result of spiritual renewal, the Holy Spirit will open your heart and release what the Lord is speaking to you. The participants will come together for several sessions, break up into small groups and share in brainstorming exercises. The information that is shared will be used to develop your action plan. Every person within the group is different and unique. Therefore, no two people will develop the same plan. However, each person should be able to make a significant contribution to this joint effort. Next, you will continue your discussion by answering the following questions to begin the formulation of your plan.

QUESTIONS FOR DISCUSSION

1. Where do you go from here regarding the millennials?

2. What can be done to make a difference in bridging the gap between the church and millennials?

3. How can you seek a fresh model to reclaim this generation?

4. Have the methods and programs of your church been assessed and updated to make sure that they are relevant for the millennial generation?

5. Has your church embraced technology and social media in the worship service and other areas in the church?

6. How can church leaders prepare other members in your church for the return of the millennial generation?

7. What types of evangelistic efforts will you use to go out and reclaim the millennials?

8. How will the church continue to grow and develop spiritually?

Michael Allison and Jude Kaye use the following chart to complete a plan of action as described in their book *Strategic Planning for Non-Profit Organizations*. Please complete the following chart using the responses to the questions answered and brainstorming sessions conducted.

Steps	Action Plan
Vision	
Goals	
Objectives	
Time Frame	
Strategies	
Procedures	
Team Members	
Resources	

Action Plan[59]

Once your Action Plan is completed, you are now ready to present it to your pastor and other leadership for review, discussion and implementation. Remember to keep praying for God's divine direction and guidance as you proceed to rescue the millennial generation and churchless back to the Kingdom of God.

Chapter Nine

Conclusion

"Now all has been heard; here is the conclusion of the matter: Fear God and keep His commandment, for this is the duty of all mankind." Ecclesiastes 12:13 (NIV)

The fact remains-- millennials who were very active as teenagers in the ministry are dropping out of church in great numbers. There are some churches that are attracting millennials but the number is small when compared to the population of that community. I have also noticed in my travels that churches who have millennial members are struggling trying to keep them active and connected. Thom Rainer, president of Life Way Christian Resources also confirms in his study that religion among the millennials is declining. Dr. Rainer indicates that,

> With fewer people attending worship services or praying with other faith adherents, it is not surprising that the religious landscape of our culture is changing with the maturation of the millennials. Millennials are the most religiously diverse Generation in our culture's history. Unsure of the afterlife and the life of Jesus, millennials present the church with a

great opportunity to engage them in conver-
sations dealing with the nature of truth and its
authority as God.[60]

Therefore, if the church endeavors to bridge the gap that
is prevalent between the churched and unchurched, you must
take a concerted effort to learn their culture and how to communicate with them.[61] As important, it is necessary that you
understand their pain, concerns, and desires. One of the many
lessons that I learned about the millennials:

Most young adults go through a search for significance, seeking to discern meaning, purpose,
and truth in life. Because their cultural context has made life incredibly complex and has
removed most of the anchors and guide post that
formerly made sense of reality, teenagers are in
a highly experimental mode and want exposure
to as many viable options as may exist.[62]

The Lord made a promise that He would give the church
a new heart. In the book of Jeremiah, it is proclaimed, "I will
give them a heart to know me, that I am Lord. They will be my
people, and I will be their God, for they will return to me with
all their heart" (Jeremiah 24:7). With this said, the church can
look forward to the millennials returning back in fellowship
and to the heart of God "thou shall also decree a thing, and it
shall be established unto thee" (Job 22:28). Just as the prodigal son returned to his father, so shall the millennials. "God
is raising them up with vision throughout the world. These
emerging leaders will be eager to follow the call of Christ.
The big question is--- whether those who are in the church will
have the vision to receive them and embrace their visions."[63]
Certainly it is our desire that the Church will see the millennials' vision. Paul explains this when he sends out a prayer for

spiritual wisdom to the faithful saints who are in Ephesus. His ultimate desire is that they will see God and the hope they have in Christ,

> *That the God of our Lord Jesus Christ, the Father of Glory may give to you a spirit of wisdom and of revelation in the knowledge of Him. I pray that the eyes of your heart may be enlightened, so that you will know what is the hope of His calling, what are the riches of the glory of His inheritance in the saints, and what is the exceeding greatness of His power toward us who believe, according to the working of His mighty power which He worked in Christ when He raised Him from the dead and seated Him at His right hand in the heavenly places, far above all principality and power and might and dominion, and every name that is named, not only in this age but also in that which is to come. And He put all things under His feet, and gave Him to be head over all things to the church, which is His body, the fullness of Him who fills all in all. (Ephesians 1:15-23)*

Paul explains to the saints how blessed they were to be called by Jesus and made holy by love. He continued to say that the Lord made a decision to adopt man into His family through Jesus Christ long time ago. Therefore, it was the blood that Jesus shed on the cross, which made them free from punishment and penalty. Not only did they receive freedom, but also God released a plan. This plan revealed how everything would eventually unite in Christ.

Hence, this prayer is certainly relevant to the church today. The Gospel of Christ when demonstrated in the shedding of His blood at the Cross "Connects us to God, ourselves, and others;

it places something alive and wonderful in our forgiven hearts that bridges the gap of separateness and joins us in life-bearing union. We now have something that has the power to change the entire course of someone else's existence."[64] Thus, in preparation to meet and reclaim millennials, the church must have the wisdom and revelation from God. You will obtain some of this wisdom from understanding the current social context in which millennials live along with their thoughts, issues, interest, beliefs, practices, fears, purpose, truth, and etc.[65] Also, it is necessary that you remain abreast of the current trends and resource data that pertains to them and how it relates to the future.

Secondly, "God desires that beyond mere head knowledge, our hearts would be changed and our lives and actions would be affected by what we learn."[66] More wisdom and inner healing will manifest as you submit your minds to be transformed by the Holy Spirit, Scripture, meditation, prayer, worship, seeking the face of God, and most of all love. "There is power within the life of every Christian waiting to be released, a power that could lead to further and deeper change, and a power within you that could help someone else connect more intimately to the heart of Christ."[67] The revelation of God is empowered throughout Scripture and provides the ingredients that you need to grow, and mature in a revived relationship with God. As you learn past lessons and the principles are incorporated, the church will renew an oneness with God, so that you will be able to follow His instructions.

The preparation of the church will culminate not by programs, deeds, or the hands of man, but through grace and by the spirit of God. "This is the word of the Lord to Zerubbabel, saying, not by might, nor by power, but by my spirit, said the Lord of hosts" (Zechariah 4:6). Nevertheless, the church will be prepared for the return of the millennials when the glory of God is manifested. "For I consider that the sufferings of this present time are not worthy to be compared with the glory which shall be revealed in us" (Romans 8:18). What is the glory of God?

"God's *glory* is defined as the manifestation of Christ's presence among His people and the magnification of His person by His people."[68] Understanding the glory of God is an essential path to the growth and maturity in the life of a believer. The dimensions of glory prepare us to receive and maintain the power and presence of God in our life. In the Old Testament, day and a fire showed God's glory in a cloud by night. "This was the symbol of God's presence and supernatural provision in the midst of His people."[69] Hence this same authority is present in the earth today and it will signify the essence of God's glory.

One last point... there is another generation hitting the scene. They are identified as being the most ethnically diverse generation. They were born between 1999 and 2015 and are called Generation Z, post millennials or iGeneration. They are the second largest generation alive today holding strong with 69 million compared to 66 million millennials. This generation is influenced by social media which allows them to connect with their friends and family 24/7. Their connection with technology will be the key to open up doors for the future. With this said, it is imperative that we take immediate action to address the concerns among the millennial generation in order to tackle upcoming matters regarding Generation Z.

In closing, when participants from your church complete this training model; it is my prayer that you will be prepared and empowered to go forth, connect, and reclaim the millennials back to the Gospel faith through God's supernatural power. One Last Point... **PLEASE DO NOT FORGET TO SHARE UNCONDITIONAL LOVE... IN ALL YOU SAY AND DO!**

Finally, within the core of millennials...contains the connecting keys to a gloried future in Jesus Christ. To God be the glory, Amen!

NOTES

Chapter 2 – National Trends

1. Wiktionary contributors, "churchless," *Wiktionary, The Free Dictionary*, http://en.wiktionary.org/wiki/churchless, (accessed January 23, 2015).
2. George Barna and David Kinnaman, *Churchless* (Carol Stream, Illinois: Tyndale House Publishers, Inc., 2014), 6.
3. Ibid, 4.
4. Ibid, 5.
5. Ibid, 8.
6. Gary Funk and Gregg Smith, "Nones on the Rise," Pew Research Center (October 9, 2012) www.pewforum.org/w 2012/10/09/Pew Report (accessed November 29, 2014).
7. Barna, Churchless, 8.
8. Funk, "Nones on the Rise."
9. George Barna, "What Millennials Want When They Visit Church," (March 3, 2015) https://www.barna.org/barna-update/Millennials/711-what (accessed January 27, 2015).
10. Rob Phillips, "Research: Millennials are Spiritually Diverse" (April 27, 2010), accessed February 26, 2015, www.lifeway.com/...Research...Millennials-are-spiritually-diverse.
11. Barna, "What Millennials Want When They Visit Church," 12.

12. Elmer Towns, Ed Stetzer and Warren Bird, *11 Innovations in the Local Church* (Ventura, CA: Regal Books, 2007), 15.

Chapter 3 - Generation Breakdown

13. Wiktionary contributors, "generations," *Wiktionary, The Free Dictionary*, http://en.wiktionary.org/wiki/Generation, (accessed January 23, 2015).
14. Matt Rosenberg, *"Names of Generations"*, (March, 2009), http://geography.com.about.com/od/population geography/ qt/generations (accessed March 31, 2015).
15. Ibid.
16. Ibid.
17. Allison Pond, Gregory Smith and Scott Clement, "Religion among the Millennials" Pew Research Center (February 17, 2010), www.pewforum.org/2010/02/17religion-among-the-Millennials (accessed November 22, 2014).
18. Ibid.
19. Barna, "Three Spiritual Journeys of Millennials." (May 9, 2013). http/www.barna.org/.../621-three-spiritual-journeys-of-millennials (accessed November 10, 2014).
20. Ibid.
21. Ibid.
22. Ibid.
23. Ibid.
24. Gregg Hamill, "Mixing and Managing Four Generations of Employees," http:/ www.fdu.edu/newspubs/magazine/05ws/Generations.htm (accessed January 6, 2015).
25. Ibid.

Chapter 4 – Lessons Learned: Why Do Millennials Drop Out?

26. Michelle C. van der Merwe and Anske F. Grobler, "Getting Young Adults Back to Church: A Marketing Approach," *AOSIS Open Journals* 69.2 (July 2013): 1, (accessed January 4, 2015).
27. Ibid.
28. Ibid.
29. Jamaal Abdul-Alim, "Why are Millennials Dropping Out?" *Diverse Issues in Higher Education* 29, no. 12 (July 19, 2012): 8-9, (accessed November 18, 2014).
30. George Barna, "Most Twenty-Somethings put Christianity on the Shelf Following Spiritually Active Teen Years." (November 16, 2014): http:/www.barna.org/FlexPage. aspx?age=BarnaUpdate&BarnaUpdateID=245.

Chapter 5 – Rescuing The Millennial Generation: What Do They Want?

31. Larry Crabb, *Connecting* (Nashville, TN: W Publishing Company, 2005), 49.
32. Jerry Bridges, *Growing Your Faith* (Colorado Springs, CO: NavPress Company, 2004), 2.

Chapter 6 – Setting the Stage: How Does the Church Move Forward?

33. Richard J. Foster, *Celebration of Discipline – The Path to Spiritual Growth* (New York, NY: Harper Collins Publishers, 1998).
34. Ibid.

Chapter 7 – Eight Keys to Spiritual Restoration

35. Barna, "Five Reasons Millennials Leave the Church."
36. Elmer L. Towns, *Worship through the Ages* (Nashville, TN: B&H Publishing Group, 2012), 136.
37. Ibid.
38. Towns, *Worship Through the Ages,* 155.
39. Erickson, *Christian Theology,* 318.
40. Ibid, 321.
41. Ibid, 322.
42. Richard J. Foster, *Prayer, Finding the Heart's True Home* (New York, NY: HarperCollins Publishers, 1992).
43. Ibid.
44. Daniel Henderson, *Fresh Encounters – Experiencing Transformation Through United Worship-Based Prayer* (Colorado Springs, CO: NavPress, 2008), 67.
45. Ibid.
46. Elmer Towns, *Praying the Lord's Prayer for Spiritual Break through* (Ventura, CA: Regal Books, 1997).
47. Ibid.
48. Towns, *Worship through the Ages,* 47.
49. Henderson, *Transforming Prayer,* 27.
50. Ibid.
51. Ibid, 5.
52. Henderson, *Transforming Prayer.*
53. Towns, *Worship through the Ages,* 49.
54. Elmer L. Towns, *Fasting for Spiritual Breakthrough,* 20.
55. Ibid.
56. Tommy Tenney, *The God Chasers* (Shippensburg, PA: Destiny Image Publishers, Inc., 1998).
57. Ibid.

Chapter 8 – What is Next: A Plan of Action

58. Erickson, *Christian Theology*, 371.
59. Michael Allison and Jude Kaye, *Strategic Planning for Nonprofit Organizations* (Hoboken, NJ: John Wiley & Sons, Inc., 2005).

Chapter 9 - Conclusion

60. Phillips, *Millennials are Spiritually Diverse*.
61. Barna, *Churchless*, 5.
62. Barna, *Real Teens* (Ventura, CA: Regal Books, 2001).
63. George Barna, *Leaders on Leadership* (Ventura, CA: Regal Books, 1997), 122.
64. Larry Crabb, *Connecting* (Nashville, TN: W Publishing Group, 1005), 6.
65. Guns, "7 Keys to Reaching the Millennial Generation," 29.
66. Ibid.
67. Crabb, *Connecting*, 7.
68. Henderson, *Fresh Encounters*, 71.
69. Ibid, 72.

BIBLIOGRAPHY

Abdul-Alim, Jamaal. "The Millennial View." *Diverse Issues in Higher Education* 29, no. 12 (July 19, 2012): 8-9. Accessed November 12, 2014. www.liberty.edu.ezproxy.liberty. edu: 2048.

Allen, Bob. "SBC baptism, membership numbers fall." *Baptist News Global* (June 6, 2013). Accessed November 5, 2014. http://www.abpnews.com/ ministry/organizations/ item / 8562.

Allison, Michael and Jude Kaye. *Strategic Planning for Nonprofit Organizations.* Hoboken, NJ: John Wiley & Sons, Inc., 2005.

Barna, George and David Kinnaman. "Three Spiritual Journeys of Millennials." (May 9, 2013). Accessed on November 10, 2014. https://www.barna. org/.../621-three-spiritual-journeys-of-millennials.

Barna, George. "Five Trends among the Unchurch." (October, 2014). Accessed December 15, 2014. http://www.barna. org/.../culture/685-five-trends-among-the-unchurched.

_____. *Revolutionary Parenting.* Ventura, CA: Regal Books, 2004.

_____. *Leaders on Leadership.* Ventura, CA: Regal Books, 1997.

_____. *Real Teens.* Ventura, CA: Regal Books, 2001.

_____. *Turn-Around Churches.* Ventura, CA: Regal Books, 1993.

Blank, Les and Mark Ballard. "Revival of hope: A critical generation for the church." *Christian Education Journal* 6, No.

2 (Fall 2002): 7fals. Accessed November 5, 2014. www. liberty.edu.ezproxy.liberty.edu:2048.

Bruce, Nolan. "Gallup reports new low in religious confidence." *Religion News Service* (July 16, 2012). Accessed November 29, 2014. www.religionnews.com/2012/07/16/ gallup-reports-new-low.

Burstein, David D. *Fast Future: How the Millennial Generation is Shaping Our World.* Cincinnati, OH: Beacon Publishers, 2013.

Clarke, Michael A. "Claiming Elijah's Mantle: Young Adults and the Life of the Church." *Anglican Theological Review*, no. 89.1(2007): 59-68.

Coomes, Michael D. Serving the Millennial Generation: New Directions for Student Services, Number 106. San Francisco, CA: Jossey Bass Wiley Publishing Company, 2004.

Couser, Tom. *Passing the Torch: Sharing Faith and Values with the Millennial Generation.* Denver, CO: Outskirts Press, Inc., 2013.

Crabb, Larry. *Connecting.* Nashville, TN: W Publishing Group, 2005.

Deitsch, Christopher. *"Creating a Millennial Generation Contextualized Church Culture."* DMin diss., Liberty University, 2012.

Dudley, Roger L. and Randall L. Wisbey. "2000.The Relationship of Parenting Styles to Commitment to the Church among Young Adults." *Religious Education*, No. 95.1: 39-51.

Egeler, Daniel. *Mentoring Millennials: Shaping the Next Generation.* Carol Stream, IL: Tyndale House Publishers, 2003.

Ender, Morten G. *The Millennial Generation and National Defense.* Australia: Palgravefalse Macmillan, 2013.

Erickson, Millard. *Christian Theology.* Grand Rapids, MI: Baker Academic, 2005.

Featherstone, Vaughn J. *The Millennial Generation: Leading Today's Youth into the Future.* New York, NY: Barnes & Noble, 1999.

Ferri-Reed, Jan. "Millennials – Generation "Screwed" or Generation "Shrewd." *The Journal for Quality and Participation,* 36, no. 1 (April 2013): 22-23. Accessed November 16, 2014.

Foster, Richard J. *Celebration of Discipline – The Path to Spiritual Growth.* New York, NY: Harper Collins Publishers, 1998.

_____. *Finding the Heart's True Home.* New York, NY: HarperCollins Publishers, 1992.

Funk, Gary and Smith. "Nones on the Rise." *Pew Research Center* (October 9, 2012). Accessed November 29, 2014. www.peewforum.org/w 2012/10/09/ Pew Report.

Grobler, Anske F. and Michelle C. van der Merwe. "Getting young adults back to church: a marketing approach." *Practical Theology of the Society* 69, No. 2 (April 2013): 1-12. Accessed November 11, 2014. http://www.hts.org.za.

Guns, Geoffrey. "7 Keys to Reaching the Millennial Generation." *The Christian Education Informer, A Journal of Christians Education,* 66, No.3 (November 2014): 28-32. Accessed February 2, 2015.

Gregg Hamill "Mixing and Managing Four Generations of Employees" Accessed January 6, 2015. http:/www.fdu.edu/newspubs/magazine/05ws/generations.htm.

Haugen, David. *Millennial Generation.* Detroit, MI: Greenhaven Press Company, 2009.

Haugen, David M. *Millennial Generation. The Opposing Viewpoints.* Detroit, MI: Greenhaven Press Company, 2012.

Henderson, Daniel. *Fresh Encounters.* Colorado Springs, CO: NavPress, 2008.

Henderson, Daniel. *Transforming Prayer.* Minneapolis, MN: Bethany House Publishers, 2011.

Hoover, Margaret. "How 9/11 Shaped the Millennial Generation and lessons for Republicans today." *Ripon Forum* 45, No. 3 (Summer 2011): 20-21. Accessed October 22, 2014. www. liberty.edu.ezproxy.liberty.edu:2048.

Howe, Neil and William Strauss. *Millennial Rising: The Next Great Generation*. New York, NY: Vintage Publishers, 2000.

Kimball, Dan. *Emerging Church*, Grand Rapids, MI: Zondervan Publishers, 2003.

Kinnaman, David. *You Lost Me*. Grand Rapids, MI: Baker Books, 2011.

Kramer, Rachelle. "Polarized Youth? The Millennial Generation, Chant, and the New Roman Missal." *Pastoral Music* 36, No. 3 (March 2012): 15-17. Accessed November 14, 2014. www.liberty.edu.ezproxy.liberty.edu:2048.

Lancaster, Lynne C. and David Stillman. *The M-Factor: How the Millennial Generation is Rocking the Workplace*. New York, NY: HarperCollins Publishing Co., 2010.

Lawrence, Dominic. *Cultivation of the Millennial Generation*. Saarbrucken, Germany: VDM Verlag Publishing Co., 2011.

Martin, A. Allan. "Burst the Bystander Effect: Making a Discipling Difference with Young Adults." *The Journal of Applied Christian Leaders,* no. 3.1 (2008/2009) 47-54.

McAllister, Dawson, *Saving the Millennial Generation*. Nashville, TN: Thomas Nelson, Inc., 2009.

Murray, Neil D. "Welcome to the future: The Millennial Generation." *Journal of Career Planning and Employment* 57, no. 3 (Spring 1997): 36-42. Accessed November 16, 2014. www.liberty.edu.ezproxy.liberty.edu:2048.h.

Pond, Allison, Gregory Smith, and Scott Clement. "Religion Among the Millennials" *Pew Research Center* (February 17, 2010). Accessed November 22, 2014. www.pewforum. org/2010/02/17/religion-among-the-millennials.

Rainer, Thom S. and Jesse Rainer. *The Millennials Connecting to America's Largest Generation*. Nashville, TN: B&H Books, 2011.

Saad, Lydia. "Rise in Religious "Nones" Slows in 2012," *Religion News* (January 13, 2013). Accessed January 4, 2015. http://www.gallup.com/poll/159785/rise-religious-nones-slows-2012.aspxt.

Scazzero, Peter and Warren Bird. *The Emotionally Healthy Church: A Strategy for Discipleship That Actually Changes Lives.* Grand Rapids, MI: Zondervan, 2003.

Smith, Paul. *The Church on the Brink.* Wheaton, Ill: Tyndale House Publishers, Inc., 1977.

Tenney, Tommy. *The God Chasers.* Shippensburg, PA: Destiny Image Publishers, Inc., 1998.

Thoman, Rick. "Mentoring: How young leaders can transform the church and why we should let them." *Christian Education Journal* 6, No. 2 (Fall 2009): 432-436. Accessed November 11, 2014. www.liberty.edu.ezproxy.liberty.edu:2048.

Towns, Elmer L. *Fasting for a Miracle.* Ventura, CA: Regal Publishing Co., 2012.

Towns, Elmer L. *How to Pray When You Don't Know What to Say.* Ventura, CA: Regal Publishing Co., 2006. Publishing Co., 2006.

_____. *Knowing God through Fasting.* Shippensburg, PA: Destiny Image Publishers, Inc., 2002.

_____. *Praying the Lord's Prayer for Spiritual Break through.* Ventura, CA: Regal Books, 1997.

_____. *Fasting for Spiritual Breakthrough.* Ventura, CA: Regal Books, 1996, 20.

Towns, Elmer L. and Daniel Henderson. *The Church That Prays Together.* Colorado Springs, CO: NavPress, 2008.

Towns, Elmer L., and Vernon Whaley. *Worship through the Ages.* Nashville, TN: B&H Publishing Group, 2012.

Towns, Elmer and Warren Bird. *Into the Future.* Grand Rapids, MI: Revell, 2000, 5.

Van der Merwe, Michelle C. and Anske F. Grobler, "Getting Young Adults Back to Church: A Marketing Approach."

AOSIS Open Journals 69.2 (July 2013): 1. Accessed January 4, 2015.

Verhaagen, David. *Parenting the Millennial Generation: Guiding Our Children born between 1982 and 2000.* Santa Barbara, CA: ABC-CLIO, Inc., 2005.

Wagner, C. Peter. *Strategies for Church Growth: Tools for Effective Mission and Evangelism.* Glendale, CA: Regal Books, 2010.

Winograd, Morley and Michael Hais. *Millennial Momentum: How a New Generation is Remaking America.* Newark, NJ: Rutgers University Press, 2011.

CPSIA information can be obtained
at www.ICGtesting.com
Printed in the USA
FFOW03n2321080218
44947942-45220FF